FUN SONGS

for the early years

Multicultural songs

Jean Evans and Sally Scott

Credits

Authors
Jean Evans and Sally Scott

Editor
Kate Element

Assistant Editor
Jennifer Howard

Series Designer
Anna Oliwa

Designer
Geraldine Reiddy

Cover Illustration
Chris Simpson

Illustrations
Louise Gardner

All songs performed by
Sally Scott
and Simon Anderson

Text © Jean Evans and Sally Scott 2006
© 2006 Scholastic Ltd

Designed using Adobe InDesign

Published by Scholastic Ltd
Villiers House
Clarendon Avenue
Leamington Spa
Warwickshire
CV32 5PR

www.scholastic.co.uk

Printed by Bell & Bain

1 2 3 4 5 6 7 8 9   6 7 8 9 0 1 2 3 4 5

British Library Cataloguing-in-Publication Data
A catalogue record for this book is available from the British Library.

ISBN 0 439 96536 5
ISBN 9 780 439 96536 1

Acknowledgement

Qualifications and Curriculum Authority for the uses of extracts from the QCA/DfEE document Curriculum Guidance for the Foundation Stage © 2000 Qualifications and Curriculum Authority.

Every effort has been made to trace copyright holders for the works reproduced in this book, and the publishers apologise for any inadvertent omissions.

Contents

Contents

Music and dance

Festivals

Introduction

Raising awareness

The songs and activities in this book have been chosen to provide a positive introduction to a wide range of cultures and faiths. They will help to provide opportunities for children to learn within an environment that celebrates and acknowledges differences.

All of the 15 lively songs on this CD have refreshing and interesting lyrics to stimulate children's interest. The practical activities that support these songs will help to raise children's multicultural awareness in a fun, simple way. Eight of the tunes will be familiar to most early years practitioners while the remaining seven have original catchy tunes that will be easy to remember.

Be led by the children's interest as they take part in these exciting experiences, and always be open-minded and willing to support them in their eagerness to make new discoveries about the diverse world in which they live.

How to use this book

There are four themed chapters relating to different aspects of multicultural awareness; Around the world, Food, Music and dance and Festivals. For each song, there are four pages. The first two provide the musical score and the song lyrics with suggested actions.

The music enables practitioners to play the tunes themselves, introducing suitable percussion accompaniment. The second two pages consist of two sections headed 'Sharing the song' and 'Activity ideas', and a photocopiable activity for each song (except the last one). 'Sharing the song' explains the learning concepts which can be developed through the song, with suggestions on how to use it to support relevant themes. 'Activity ideas' suggests activities to follow up the song's concepts and themes. The main activity idea for each song has been given a learning objective, consisting of a Stepping Stone and an Early Learning Goal. The book provides a good balance across all Areas of Learning of the Foundation Stage (see box below for shorthand used).

Involving the children

Introduce each song by playing the CD, several times if possible, inviting the children to join in with the words while they copy your actions. It is important to encourage the children to enjoy the CD independently in child-initiated play as well as during adult-led activities. So, demonstrate how to use a CD player safely so that the children can operate it independently.

Create 'theme boxes' for associated cultures, for example, an 'Australian box' so that children can explore books and artefacts before or after playing the song 'In Australia!' on their CD player.

Produce interactive displays related to a specific culture or festival so that children can investigate resources and explore posters. For example, create a kite flying area for children to visit after listening independently to 'Kodomo-no-hi', with a wall display about kite flying and a table of simple kite-making resources.

Provide the children with percussion instruments so that they can play along to the songs.

Areas of Learning

PSED Personal, social and emotional education
CLL Communication, language and literacy
MD Mathematical development
KUW Knowledge and understanding of the world
PD Physical development
CD Creative development

Around the world

in Australia!

Koa-la bears climb up the trees, up the trees, up the trees. Koa-la bears climb up the trees, In Au-stra-li-a!

Sally Scott

In Australia!

(The children divide into four groups representing koala bears, kangaroos, crocodiles and emus, each group sitting in a different corner of a large floor space.)

Koala bears climb up the trees,
up the trees, up the trees.
Koala bears climb up the trees,
In Australia!

(The koala bear group stand up and pretend to climb trees while the other children sing the song.)

Kangaroos hop through the fields,
through the fields, through the fields.
Kangaroos hop through the fields,
In Australia!

(The kangaroo group stand up and pretend to hop through the fields using all of the available floor space while the other children sing the song.)

Crocodiles hide in the lakes,
in the lakes, in the lakes.
Crocodiles hide in the lakes,
In Australia!

(The crocodile group crawl around the available floor space until they find an imaginary hiding place well away from the others while the seated children sing the song.)

Emus run, they cannot fly,
cannot fly, cannot fly.
Emus run, they cannot fly.
In Australia!

(The emu group stand up and run around using all of the available floor space while the other children sing the song.)

In Australia!
How to use this song

Learning objectives

Stepping Stone
Observe the effects of activity on their bodies.

Early Learning Goal
Recognise the changes that happen to their bodies when they are active. **(PD)**

Group size
Large group (16 children).

Props
Small plastic models and large pictures of koala bears, kangaroos, crocodiles and emus; globe.

Sharing the song

Share this song with the children during a music and movement session, or use it as a planned activity to support themes such as 'Australia', 'countries of the world' and 'living things'.

Before singing the song initially, pass around the plastic models and look at the pictures. Introduce the names of these creatures if necessary and explain that they live a country called Australia. Find Australia on a globe and move a finger around to where the children live. How would they travel to Australia?

Hold up a model of each creature in turn and talk about how it might move. Use the words of the song, such as 'climb', 'hop' and 'run', to help. How might a crocodile move with its short scaly legs? Explore different ways of imitating the creatures in the song and then put these movements into action while singing.

Once the children are familiar with the creatures and their country of origin omit these initial discussions. With younger children, or smaller groups, have the children create actions for all of the verses instead of dividing them into groups. Sing the song several times so that the children can pretend to be different creatures.

After taking part in the song, invite the children to rest and to talk to the rest of the group about the changes they feel in their bodies after their exercise.

Activity ideas

● Make copies of the pictures of the creatures on page 9, mount them on card and cut them out. Ask the children to turn all of the cards upside down and then take turns to pick up two to try to make a pair. If the two cards do not match, return them to the same place. The aim is for each child to collect as many pairs as possible. Use the cards as prompts for the children as they move like the different creatures. **(PSED)**

● Invite the children to help you to make a book about Australia. Include pictures of famous landmarks and buildings, such as Ayers rock, Sydney Opera House and Sydney Harbour Bridge and invite the children to create drawings of Australian animals and birds, such as kangaroos, koalas, emus and crocodiles. **(CLL)**

● Look at Australian artefacts such as a boomerang, cork hat and didgeridoo. Have fun throwing home-made boomerangs in wide open spaces, making cork hats and creating didgeridoos from plastic pipes. **(KUW)**

● Explore Aboriginal art, such as dot and bark paintings, and suggest that the children create their own designs based on these forms. Include them in a home-made book about Australia (see activity above). **(CD)**

In Australia!

In Mexico!

Look — how — they dance, Look — how they dance. They — dance the sal - sa, they — dance the sal - sa. Look how — they dance, look — how they dance. They — dance the sal - sa in — Me - xi - co! In Me - xi - co —, In Me - xi - co —! In Me - xi - co —, In Me - xi - co —!

Sally Scott

In Mexico!

(The children choose from a selection of colourful shawls and ponchos to wear over their shoulders representing Mexican clothing. Four of them then stand to the side of the dance area carrying maracas in each hand while the remaining children move to the middle of the floor.)

Look how they dance, look how they dance.
They dance the salsa, they dance the salsa.
Look how they dance, look how they dance.
They dance the salsa, in Mexico!

(The maraca players accompany the music while the others follow the beat and move freely to the music. All of the children sing the words of the song.)

In Mexico, in Mexico!
In Mexico, in Mexico!

(The maraca players continue to accompany the music.)

Look what they eat, look what they eat.
Eat enchiladas, eat enchiladas!
Look what they eat, look what they eat.
Eat enchiladas, in Mexico!

(The maraca players accompany the music while the others mime eating a hot and spicy enchilada, waving a hand across their mouths to cool themselves down. All of the children continue to sing.)

In Mexico, in Mexico!
In Mexico, in Mexico!

(The maraca players continue to accompany the music.)

Look what they wear, look what they wear.
Sombrero hats, sombrero hats!
Look what they wear, look what they wear.
Sombrero hats, in Mexico!

(The maraca players accompany the music while the others move to the side of the area and put on a sombrero before continuing to dance and sing.)

In Mexico, in Mexico!
In Mexico, in Mexico!

(The maraca players continue to accompany the music.)

In Mexico!
How to use this song

Learning objectives

Stepping Stone
Respond to sound with body movement.

Early Learning Goal
Recognise repeated sounds and sound patterns and match movements to music. **(CD)**

Group size
12 children.

Props
Pictures of Mexican people wearing traditional dress such as sombreros, rebozo (colourful shawls), ponchos and serapes (blankets worn over the shoulder); eight maracas; colourful lengths of fabric; simple home-made child-sized ponchos; sombreros, or sun hats with a wide brim.

Sharing the song

Share this song with the children at circle time before a discussion about Mexican life, or during a dance session. Link the song to planned activities supporting different aspects of themes such as 'countries of the world', 'food' and 'clothes'.

Before singing the song, look at pictures of traditional Mexican dress together and name the garments. Introduce the lengths of fabric and home-made ponchos and suggest that the children choose something they would like to wear as they sing and dance. Explain what is meant by an enchilada, referring to something within the child's experience such as a tortilla, fajita or pancake.

Listen to the song and invite the children to clap the rhythm, explaining that this is a Mexican salsa beat. Have the children ever heard of salsa dancing? Invite them to dress in their choice of Mexican clothing and make up their own salsa dance to the instrumental version of the song. Suggest that four of the children play maracas to emphasise the rhythm.

Once the children are familiar with the Mexican aspects of the song omit these introductory discussions.

Always be willing to try any new ideas the children might have, for example, to play an alternative instrument as accompaniment or to wear different dressing up clothes.

Activity ideas

● Follow the recipe on page 13 to make some enchiladas or tortillas to share at snack time. Encourage the children to choose their own fillings and talk about their taste preferences. Remember to gain permission for the children to taste food and to check for any food allergies. **(PSED)**

● Convert the home area into a Mexican house by draping the sides with white sheeting printed with brick shapes in a terracotta colour. Supply colourful fabrics for rebozo, serapes and ponchos and some wide-brimmed hats. **(CLL)**

● Talk about how Mexicans love wearing coloured beads and make some beads from clay balls with a hole pierced through the centre. Bake and then paint in different colours and varnish. Thread the beads onto lengths of string in sequences to create repeat patterns. **(MD)**

● Obtain a recording of the Mexican Hat Dance, a very fast tune played on a guitar, traditionally danced by couples wearing Mexican dress. Play it for the children and have fun wearing large hats and making up your own hat dances. **(PD)**

In Mexico!

1. Mix together:
200g wholemeal flour
50g margarine
120ml water.

2. Knead to form a dough.

3. Roll the mixture into 10 balls and allow to stand for 15 minutes.

4. Roll out the balls into pancake shapes.

5. Cook the tortillas in oil in a frying pan away from the children.

6. Add fillings, for example, chopped tomatoes, onion, mushroom, garlic, sour cream, pinch of chilli powder, grated cheese.

7. Roll up and enjoy tasting together.

Rain Dance

Em

Pi - tter pa - tter. Pi - tter pa - tter. Pi - tter pa - tter. Pi - tter pa - tter. Rain

drops! Can you hear the, can you hear the Pi - tter pa - tter. Pi - tter pa - tter.

Rain drops fa - - - lling.

Pi - tter pa - tter. Pi - tter pa - tter. Pi - tter pa - tter. Pi - tter pa - tter.

Rain drops fa - - lling down.

Sally Scott

Rain Dance

(Children remove their shoes and socks and top garments such as cardigans and sweatshirts. Four children hold rainsticks and drums ready to accompany the song.)

Pitter patter, pitter patter,
Pitter patter, pitter patter.
Rain drops!

(Four children sit playing rainsticks and drums to accompany the song while the others kneel on the floor in a circle around them and bend up and down, waving their arms straight in front of them while wiggling their fingers to represent rain falling.)

Can you hear the, can you hear the,
Pitter patter, pitter patter,
Rain drops falling.
Pitter patter, pitter patter,
Pitter patter, pitter patter.
Rain drops falling down.

(The four children continue to play their instruments while the others drum their fingers on the ground to make the sound of raindrops falling.)

(When the song is repeated the children around the edge of the circle stand up and invent their own rain dances to the music. Encourage them to think about the speed of their movements, for example, moving quickly in time to the words 'pitter patter' and more slowly to 'rain drops'.)

Rain Dance
How to use this song

Learning objectives

Stepping Stone
Have a positive approach to new experiences.

Early Learning Goal
Continue to be interested, excited and motivated to learn. **(PSED)**

Group size
12 children.

Props
A selection of home-made and commercially produced rainsticks and drums (see activity ideas).

Sharing the song

Share this song with the children during a music and dance session, or link it to planned activities supporting themes such as 'sound', 'my body' and 'countries of the world'.

Explain how some people, such as Native American Indians and Africans, make their own drums to send messages across distances by beating out different rhythms and invent dances to encourage rain to fall.

Listen to the song and decide upon appropriate finger, hand and arm movements to indicate raindrops falling. Suggest 'drumming' fingers on the ground to make additional sound effects.

Listen to the sound made by rainsticks. Try out the different drums and decide which ones sound most like rain. Invite four children to choose instruments from the selection and ask them to sit in a group. Encourage the others to sit in a circle around them.

Next, sing the song and add the practised movements and percussion. When the song is repeated, ask the children around the circle to make up rain dances in time to the music while the others play instruments and sing.

Activity ideas

● Read the book *Handa's Surprise* by Eileen Browne (Walker Books) and explain that African people often carry things on their heads, just like Handa. Invite the children to try balancing small blankets on their heads. **(CLL)**

● Show the children a picture of a tepee and explain that American Indians make their homes in them. Make copies of page 17 and mount them on card. Invite the children to create patterns on the surface of the teepee with felt pens, cut it out following the thick black lines and make folds along the dotted lines. Stand the teepees in a group to make a village for small world people. **(KUW)**

● Make a rainstick from a cardboard tube. Seal it at one end, add some rice grains and thread cocktail sticks at intervals along it. Trim the sticks and seal the other end. Explore a variety of everyday objects, such as buckets and cartons, to create drums. **(PD)**

● Explain how African people often wear masks during their rain dances and invite the children to make some from paper plates. Cut out elongated holes for eyes, a nose and a mouth, and punch holes around the edge of the plate with a hole puncher. Fasten raffia or wool strands to the holes and use elastic to hold the mask in place. **(CD)**

Rain Dance

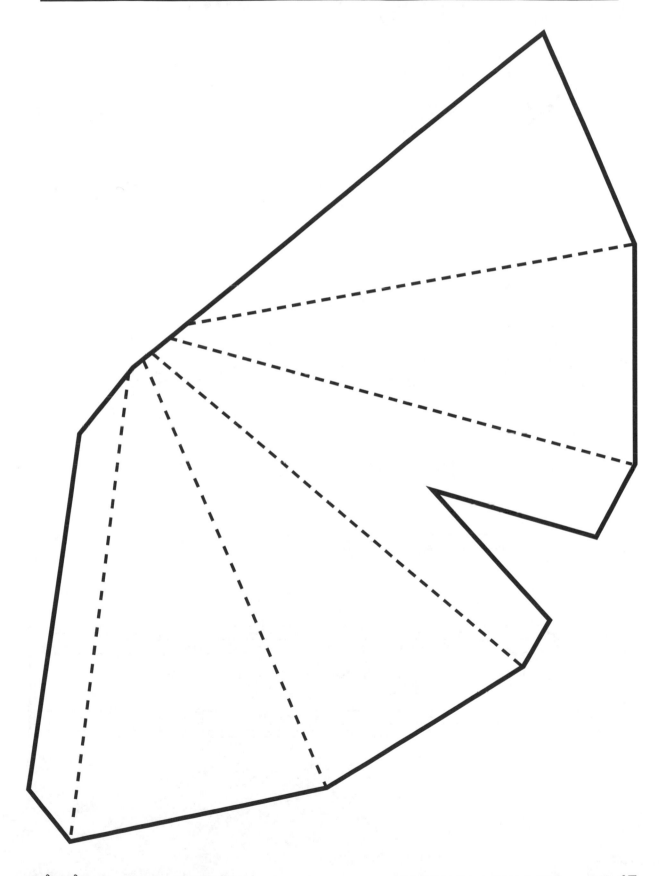

Spray Your Paint

Sally Scott

Spray Your Paint

(The children stand in a circle. Two children are chosen to play the parts of Krishna and Radha, standing opposite one another in the circle wearing white paint splattered shirts and carrying empty ready-mix paint bottles.)

Red and yellow paint, spray it all around,
Watch the colours mix and drip and run across the ground.

(All of the children pretend to spray paint around with an imaginary squeezy bottle.)

Krishna, spray your paint, having lots of fun,
Radha, Radha, run away, see the colours run!

(Krishna and Radha run into the centre of the circle. Krishna pretends to chase Radha and spray her with paint, running out of the circle and around the outside of the children before joining the circle again for the next verse.)

Blue and purple paint, spray it all around,
Watch the colours mix and drip and run across the ground.
Krishna, spray your paint, having lots of fun,
Radha, Radha, run away, see the colours run!

(Actions as first verse.)

Pink and yellow paint, spray it all around,
Watch the colours mix and drip and run across the ground.
Krishna, spray your paint, having lots of fun,
Radha, Radha, run away, see the colours run!

(Actions as first verse.)

Spray Your Paint
How to use this song

Learning objectives

Stepping Stone
Gain an awareness of the cultures and beliefs of others.

Early Learning Goal
Begin to know about their own cultures and beliefs and those of other people. **(KUW)**

Group size
12 children.

Props
Two large white shirts with the sleeves cut short, splattered with paint of all colours; two empty ready-mix paint bottles.

Sharing the song

Share this song with the children during the Hindu festival of Holi (3 March 2007, date varies from year to year) or when enjoying ring games. Link it to planned activities supporting themes such as 'colours', 'festivals' and 'changes'.

Before singing the song initially, read the story about Lord Krishna and his friend Radha on page 21. Talk about how they used to tease one another, and make links between this story and the custom of throwing paint on one another during the Hindu festival of Holi.

Explain that children celebrating Holi sometimes use sprays and squeezy bottles to spray the paint, and sometimes throw dry powder paint.

Show the children the paint splattered shirts made earlier (see activity ideas), and ask two of them to wear them to play the parts of Krishna and Radha. Sit in a circle to listen to the song and discuss the words before standing up to sing and follow the suggested actions. Repeat the song several times so that the children can take turns to be Krishna and Radha.

Activity ideas

● On a fine day, dress the children in waterproof clothes and take them outside. Have fun spraying coloured water over one another using unused plant spray bottles and squeezy bottles. **(PSED)**

● Suggest transforming the home area into a Hindu home with appropriate music playing, saris to wear and traditional utensils to use for imaginary meals. Explain how Hindu families spring clean their homes in preparation for the festival of Holi and supply the children with brushes, dustpans, dusters and cloths so that they can clean and tidy their setting. **(CLL)**

● Hang two white shirts on an outdoor fence or washing line and invite the children to spray the front of them with watery paint using unused plant spray bottles and squeezy bottles. Turn the shirts around and do the same with the back. Use the paint-splattered shirts as props for the song. Create a 'Holi' frieze by doing the same to paper shirts and attaching them to paper outlines of the children's bodies. **(PD)**

● Encourage the children to cut out people from mail order catalogues and glue them to sheets of dark coloured paper. Suggest splattering or flicking paint over their characters. Invite the children to do the same with another colour and to observe what happens when the two colours mix. Vary the activity by putting glue on the characters' bodies and sprinkling coloured glitter over them. **(CD)**

Spray Your Paint

The story of Lord Krishna and Princess Radha
retold by Jean Evans

A long time ago in India there lived a special little boy called Lord Krishna. This little boy loved to play tricks on his friends and was full of mischief.

One day he hid their clothes while they were swimming in the river and hung them up in the trees so that his friends could not reach them. Then he sat down and began to play his flute, waiting for his friends to come searching for their clothes. They jumped up and down laughing and trying to reach the branches until Krishna decided to get them down for them.

Krishna's best friend was called Radha. She was a very pretty girl with long shiny hair and the two friends spent lots of time playing together.

One night, Radha was dancing with her friends by the river in the moonlight while Krishna played his flute. All of the girls wore colourful clothes that whirled around as they danced. Radha began to sing in her beautiful voice and the people heard her and came out of their houses to listen and watch the dancing.

Then Krishna had an idea for a trick to play on his friends. He put down his flute and went off into the darkness to find lots of pots of coloured powder. Radha stopped dancing and singing and came to see what Krishna was doing. He waited quietly until she came closer and then, quick as a flash, he jumped out and threw some red powder at her. Radha giggled as her clothes began to turn red and Krishna carried on dipping his hand in the pots and throwing more and more colours.

Then Radha decided to try the same trick on Krishna and picked some powder out of a pot to throw at him. Soon there was paint everywhere, swirling round and round just like the clothes of the dancers. Before long all of the friends were throwing paint over each other, laughing together as they joined in the fun.

Ever since that day, people have been throwing coloured powder at each other during the festival of 'Holi' to remember the fun that Krishna, Radha and their friends had by the river.

Food

Brixton Market

G **C** **D** **G** **C** **D**

Let's all go down to Brix- ton mar-ket. Come with me let's go to-day ___.

G **Am** **A** **D**
spoken

Don't stop, we can shop un- til it gets dark *It's mar-ket day to-day ___!* You can buy

G

man-go ___ es. You can buy fresh co-co-nu ___ ts. And

spoken

if you're fee-ling si-lly, you can try some chi-lli. Oo, *ah, oo, ah, oo that's hot!*

Simon Anderson

Brixton Market

(Children hold hands and walk round in a circle wearing coloured fabrics of their choice.)

Let's all go down to Brixton market,
come with me let's go today.
Don't stop, we can shop until it gets dark,
It's market day today!

(Children stand still and stop holding hands before pretending to pick up things from a market stall and hand over money to an imaginary stall holder.)

You can buy mangoes, you can buy fresh coconuts,
And if you're feeling silly, you can try some chilli.
Oo, ah, oo, ah, oo, that's hot!

(Children wave a hand in front of their mouths as they pretend to cool themselves down after eating hot chillies.)

Let's all go down to Brixton market,
come with me let's go today.
Don't stop, we can shop until it gets dark,
It's market day today!

You can buy mangoes, you can buy fresh coconuts,
But don't be in a hurry, to try the chicken curry,
Oo, ah, oo, ah, oo, that's hot!

(Actions as for first verse.)

Mangoes, you can buy fresh coconuts,

(Children pretend to pick up mangoes and coconuts from a market stall and hand over money to an imaginary stall holder.)

Come along with me and we can buy something for tea,
It's market day today!

(Children hold hands again and walk round in a circle, stopping at the end of the song.)

Brixton Market
How to use this song

Sharing the song

Share this song just before lunch or snack time to stimulate discussion about food preferences, and link to themes such as 'foods from around the world', 'shopping' and 'senses'.

Invite the children to sit and listen to the song and then ask what they think the song is about. Have they ever visited a market? What did they buy? Explain that Brixton is a large market in London.

Ask the children to choose some attractive fabric to drape themselves in and then move their bodies in time to the beat as you play the song again. Sing the song together, adding the children's own actions and movements.

Suggest that the children try chanting 'oo', 'ah', 'oo', 'ah' instead of singing the words. What sounds are they making? Can they hear these sounds in words such as 'food' and 'farm'?

Ask some children to create a percussion accompaniment with appropriate multicultural instruments while the others sing.

Activity ideas

● Ask the children to listen carefully while you read out the words of the song and then draw their attention to words which sound the same, such as 'hurry' and 'curry', 'silly' and 'chilli'. Introduce the word 'rhyme' and try chanting the rhyming words together. **(PSED)**

● Set up a role-play market stall selling imitation exotic fruits and vegetables made from salt dough or papier mache. Price the items from 1p to 5p and supply the children with 1p plastic coins. Encourage the children to count out the correct number of coins for each item purchased. **(MD)**

● Visit a local market and buy a selection of fruits and vegetables from around the world. Look at the stickers to identify the country of origin and find them on a world map. Explain that Brixton is in London and point to the position of London on the map. Consider how the produce will be transported across the world to Brixton. **(KUW)**

● Make copies of the market stall picture on page 25 and encourage the children to pretend to be assistants to the market stallholder. Invite them to identify and label the items on sale by cutting out the name labels at the bottom of the page and sticking them to the picture in the correct position. **(PD)**

● Have a sensory session so that the children can handle, taste and smell a range of familiar and unusual fruits. Remember to check for any food allergies the children may have. **(CD)**

Brixton Market

yam

papaya

coconut

banana

mango

Help Me Make a Pizza

Help me make a pi - zza, a pi - zza for my tea.

First mix the dough and knead it just for me. Then

roll it and press it and put it on a tray. And

when it is cooked you can take a slice a - way!

Sally Scott

Help Me Make a Pizza

(The children sit in a circle on the floor. A child or adult is standing beside a table ready to lift up appropriate props to act as memory aids as the song progresses.)

Help me make a pizza, a pizza for my tea.
First mix the dough and knead it just for me.

(The prompt holds up a bowl. The children make the arm and hand movements necessary to mix and knead a lump of dough.)

Then roll it and press it and put it on a tray.

(The prompt holds up a rolling pin. The children pretend to roll out the dough, lift it and put it on a tray, pressing it down firmly.)

And when it is cooked you can take a slice away!

(The prompt holds up a plastic pizza. The children pretend to pick up a slice of pizza and eat it.)

Help me make a pizza, a pizza for my tea.
Next add the sauce and spread it just for me.

(The prompt holds up a plastic sauce bottle. The children pretend to put sauce onto the pizza.)

Spoon it and spread it and put it on a tray.

(The prompt holds up a spoon and baking tray. The children pretend to spread the sauce around.)

And when it is cooked you can take a slice away!

Help me make a pizza, a pizza for my tea.
Next add the toppings, toppings just for me.
Mushrooms and onions, put it on a tray.

(The prompt holds up a plastic mushroom and onion. The children pretend to sprinkle toppings on their pizza.)

And when it is cooked you can take a slice away!

(Children pretend to take and eat a slice of pizza.)

Help me make a pizza, a pizza for my tea.
Next add the cheese and grate it just for me.

(The prompt holds up a plastic cheese grater. The children pretend to grate cheese.)

Sprinkle the cheese and put it on a tray.

(The children pretend to sprinkle cheese onto their pizzas.)

And when it is cooked you can take a slice away!

(Children pretend to take and eat a slice of pizza.)

Help Me Make a Pizza
How to use this song

Learning objectives

Stepping Stone
Take initiative and manage developmentally appropriate tasks.

Early Learning Goal
Select and use activities and resources independently. **(PSED)**

Group size
Up to eight children.

Props
Imitation pizza; large bowl; baking tray; rolling pin; empty tomato sauce bottle; mushroom; onion; cheese grater; world map. (Make sure that all resources are safe for children to handle and have no sharp edges.)

Sharing the song

Share this song just before lunch to stimulate conversation about favourite foods, and link to themes such as 'foods from around the world', 'all about me' and 'changes'.

Discuss the children's experiences of enjoying a pizza. Explain that pizza is an Italian dish and look for Italy on a world map.

Describe how pizza is made with a dough base and then toppings are added before it is baked in the oven. Listen to the words of the song together and then take each verse in turn to describe the sequence of pizza making. Look at the utensils used as props, name them and talk about how they might be used. These initial discussions can be omitted once the children are familiar with where pizzas are from and how they are made.

Choose someone to act as 'prompt', holding up each utensil during appropriate verses of the song. Explain the meaning of the words used, such as 'knead' and 'toppings', and decide upon appropriate actions indicated by the movement words in each verse.

Enjoy singing the song together, adding actions and watching the prompt for support with the sequence of verses.

Activity ideas

● Invite the children to make pictorial pizza recipe cards, naming and illustrating their personal choice of toppings. Encourage them to tell the rest of the group about their choices. **(CLL)**

● Make copies of photocopiable page 29, mount them on card and cut out the individual pizza shapes to create a matching card game. Play the game to develop children's awareness of patterns and two-dimensional shapes. **(MD)**

● Follow a simple recipe for a pizza dough, or buy some ready made bases, and provide each child with a small base. Encourage them to spread this with tomato sauce and choose from a selection of toppings to arrange on top. Finally grate cheese all over it and put it in the oven to cook. Encourage the children to observe and discuss changes in the various ingredients as they are heated. Remember to check for any allergies before allowing the children to taste food. **(KUW)**

● Make a large pizza base from cardboard and spread it with tomato puree made from red paint thickened with paste. Invite the children to stick on toppings created from art and collage materials, for example, fabric mushrooms, yellow wool grated cheese, sponge pineapple pieces and pepperoni made from buttons. Suggest using the pizza as a prop for the song. **(CD)**

Help Me Make a Pizza

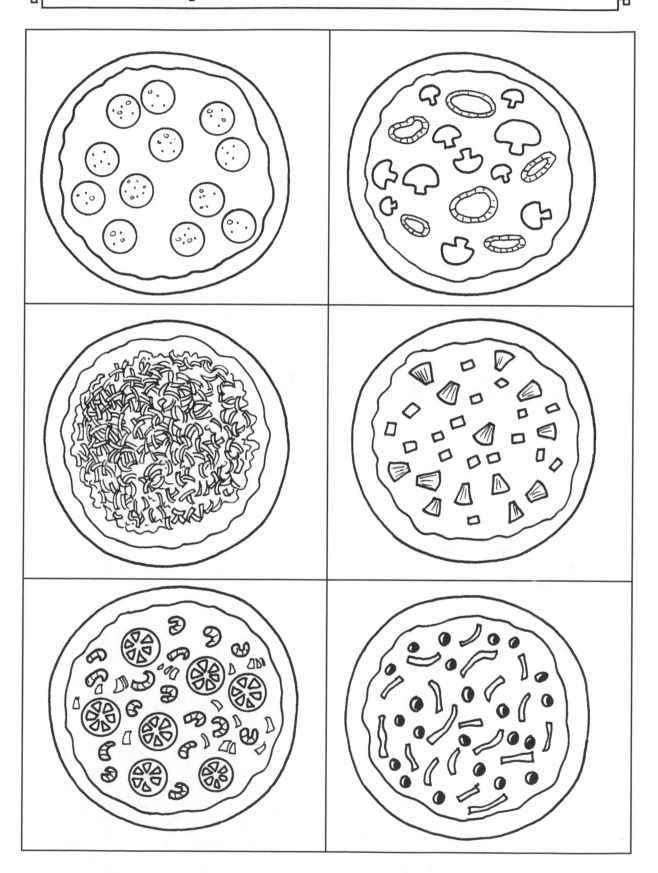

Growing in My Garden

Five ears of corn are grow-ing in my gar-den. Five ears of corn are

grow-ing in my gar-den. I'm going to pick them and cook them in a pot. And

I'm going to eat them, eat them whilst they're hot!

Sally Scott

Growing in My Garden

(Five children stand in a line holding up the prop cards for the song in order, from five ears of corn down to to one Chinese cabbage. One child stands alongside.)

Five ears of corn are growing in my garden.
Five ears of corn are growing in my garden.

(The child holding the 'ears of corn' card holds it high in the air.)
I'm going to pick them and cook them in a pot.
And I'm going to eat them, eat them whilst they're hot!
(The child standing to the side of the others pretends to pick ears of corn from the child holding up the card and then eat them. The child with the card sits down.)

Four aubergines are growing in my garden.
Four aubergines are growing in my garden.
(The child holding the 'aubergines' card holds it high in the air.)
I'm going to pick them and cook them in a pot.
And I'm going to eat them, eat them whilst they're hot!

(As for the first verse, with the child picking aubergines this time.)

Three sweet potatoes are growing in my garden.
Three sweet potatoes are growing in my garden.

(The child holding the 'sweet potatoes' card holds it high in the air.)
I'm going to pick them and cook them in a pot.
And I'm going to eat them, eat them whilst they're hot!

(As for the first verse, but with the child picking sweet potatoes.)

Two artichokes are growing in my garden.
Two artichokes are growing in my garden.
(The child holding the 'artichokes' card holds it high in the air.)
I'm going to pick them and cook them in a pot.
And I'm going to eat them, eat them whilst they're hot!

(As for the first verse, but with the child picking artichokes.)

One Chinese cabbage is growing in my garden.
One Chinese cabbage is growing in my garden.
(The child holding the 'Chinese cabbage' card holds it high in the air.)
I'm going to pick it and cook it in a pot.
And I'm going to eat it, eat it whilst it's hot!

(As for the first verse, but with the child picking a Chinese cabbage. The remaining child sits down and the cards are swapped around before repeating the song.)

Growing in My Garden
How to use this song

Learning objectives

Stepping Stone
Find the total number of items in two groups by counting all of them.

Early Learning Goal
Begin to relate addition to combining two groups of objects and subtraction to 'taking away'. **(MD)**

Group size
Six children.

Props
Five cards depicting pictures or drawings of five ears of corn, four aubergines, three sweet potatoes, two artichokes and one Chinese cabbage, with the appropriate numeral displayed clearly above the illustration; one example of each of the vegetables.

Sharing the song

Share this song in the number area or during a group discussion to stimulate number recognition and counting skills, and link to themes such as 'foods from around the world', 'senses' and 'growing'.

Before listening to the song plan a session where the children can handle the vegetables mentioned. Tell the children the vegetable names and countries of origin and encourage them to talk about how they look, smell and feel. Keep them to one side for a tasting session later (see activity ideas).

Look at the cards together and try to match each one to the correct vegetable. Spend time counting the number of vegetables on each card and arranging the cards in order along the floor from one to five. Choose a child to pretend to eat the

vegetables at the end of each verse and invite the others to take turns to go and stand by a card so that everyone has a part to play in the song. Sing the song together, following the suggested actions, or making up actions of your own.

After singing the song spend time counting combinations of the vegetables depicted on the cards, and extend this by introducing the mathematical activity explained below.

Activity ideas

● Help the children chop up and cook the vegetables in separate pans. Taste each one in turn and make comparisons. Invite the children to say which one they like best and least. Emphasise that it is fine to have differing likes and dislikes. **(PSED)**

● Provide each child with a copy of the picture on page 33. Identify the different types of vegetables and count the number in each row. Cover each vegetable with a counter of an appropriate colour, such as yellow for corn and purple for aubergines. Pose simple problems involving adding up different combinations of counters, for example, 'If I have four aubergines and one Chinese cabbage, how many vegetables do I have altogether?'. **(MD)**

● Set up a vegetable plot outdoors, or sow some seeds in indoor pots, and encourage the children to tend their vegetables regularly. Choose a combination of familiar and more exotic vegetables. **(KUW)**

Growing in My Garden

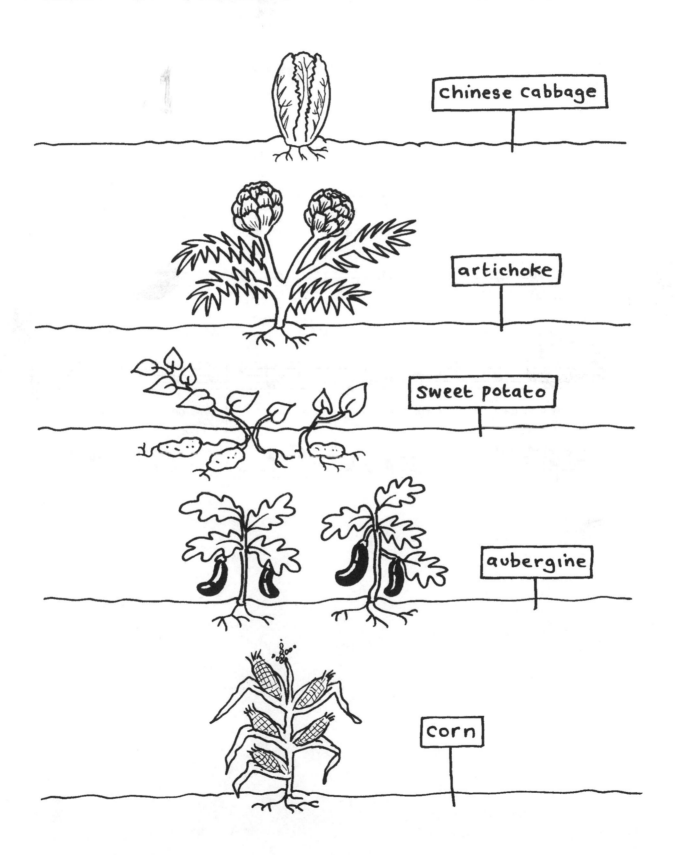

chinese cabbage

artichoke

sweet potato

aubergine

corn

Music and dance

Lion Dance

Now watch me do the li - on dance, li - on dance,

li - on dance. Now watch me do the li - on dance, li - on dance!

Sally Scott

Lion Dance

(Four children dance as two pairs, each with one child holding a lion's head mask and the other bending over and holding onto the back of the mask holder so that each pair can pretend to be a lion dancing. One child teases the two lions by waving a fan. Three children act as the musicians playing a large drum, cymbals and a gong who play their instruments throughout the song.)

Now watch me do the lion dance,
lion dance, lion dance.
Now watch me do the lion dance,
lion dance!

(A child teases the lions by waving a fan and the 'lions' make up a dance around the teasing child)

Now watch me shake my lion mask,
lion mask, lion mask.
Now watch me do the lion dance,
lion dance!

(The two children representing the lions' heads shake their masks by lifting up the sticks they are holding and waving them from side to side in front of the teasing child.)

Now watch me jump like lions jump,
lions jump, lions jump.
Now watch me do the lion dance,
lion dance!

(The 'lions' jump up and down in front of the teasing child.)

Now watch me roar like lions roar,
lions roar, lions roar.
Now watch me do the lion dance,
lion dance!

(The 'lions' roar at the teasing child.)

Now watch me run like lions run,
lions run, lions run.
Now watch me do the lion dance,
lion dance!

(The 'lions' run around in circles in front of the teasing child.)

Now watch me do the lion dance,
lion dance, lion dance.
Now watch me do the lion dance,
lion dance!

(As first verse.)

Lion Dance
How to use this song

Learning objectives

Stepping Stone
Realise tools can be used for a purpose.

Early Learning Goal
Select the tools and techniques they need to shape, assemble and join materials they are using. **(KUW)**

Group size
Eight children.

Props
Two lion masks and tabards (see activity ideas); Chinese dressing-up clothes or a pair of plain children's pyjamas; large drum; pair of cymbals or pan lids with smooth edges; gong or metal tray; beater or stick with padded tip; fan or giant ball.

Sharing the song

Share this song during a movement and dance session, or as part of Chinese New Year celebrations (the exact date changes each year but it is between late January and mid-February). Include the song in planned activities related to themes such as 'festivals', 'celebrations', 'music from around the world', 'wild animals' and 'China'.

Explain to the children that Chinese people dress as lions and invent lion dances as part of their New Year festivities, or during celebrations such as weddings, to frighten away bad things and bring luck and happiness to everyone. Describe how the dance involves someone teasing a lion with a fan or giant ball and suggest that the children make up their own lion dance following this Chinese tradition.

Show the children the instruments and talk about the sounds they make. Explain that these are the instruments played during the Chinese lion dances and choose three children to be musicians.

Invite one of the children, dressed in Chinese dressing-up clothes or a pair of plain pyjamas, to tease the lions. Dress the remaining four children as two lions with the costumes they have created (see activity ideas).

Enjoy the dance, following the suggested actions, singing and playing instruments. Repeat the song several times so that the children can be musicians, lion teasers and lions.

Activity ideas

● Read the story on page 37 which explains how the Chinese years are named after animals. Follow this by singing the song and enjoying some special Chinese snacks. **(CLL)**

● Create your own Chinese lion dance costumes. Make a larger than life mask from thick cardboard and mark the position of the eyes, ears, nose and mouth. Use brightly coloured ribbons, foil, tissue and fabric to decorate the mask and attach two sticks to hold it, one at each side. Create a simple yellow 'body' tabard, attach a long fabric tail and sew or tie strands of coloured wool all over the surface. **(KUW)**

● Show the children some pictures of Chinese acrobats and talk about their excellent balancing skills. Pretend to be acrobats, balancing beanbags on different parts of the body. **(PD)**

● Taste some Chinese food and then set up a role-play Chinese restaurant with Chinese music, lanterns, menus and utensils. Remember to check for any food allergies that the children might have. **(CD)**

Lion Dance

The origins of the Chinese New Year
Retold by Jean Evans

This story happened a long, long time ago in China. It was nearly the end of the old year and the New Year was about to begin. Twelve animals all wanted the New Year to be named after them and so they began to have a big argument about which one of them should be chosen. They shouted so loudly that the king heard them and wondered why they were making such a noise. His daughter, the princess, also heard the noise and said to her father 'Don't worry, Father, I will go and find out what is upsetting the animals.'

She followed the sound of shouting and soon found the angry animals.

'Dear animals, what is upsetting you so?' asked the princess.

'I think that the New Year should be named after me,' roared the tiger.

'After me,' squeaked the rat.
'After me,' bellowed the ox.
'After me,' sniffled the rabbit.
'After me,' fumed the dragon.
'After me,' hissed the snake.
'After me,' neighed the horse.
'After me,' baa-ed the ram.
'After me,' chattered the monkey.
'After me,' crowed the rooster.
'After me,' barked the dog.
'After me,' snorted the pig.

'Oh dear! You cannot all have the New Year named after you,' smiled the princess. 'I think you should have a swimming race across the river. The New Year will be named after the winner.'

'What a clever idea,' chorused all of the animals. They stood in a line along the river bank until the princess shouted, 'Ready, steady, go!'.

In they jumped with a tremendous splash. The water swirled and whirled as they swam with all their strength. Soon the ox was leading, but quietly, without anyone noticing, the rat climbed up onto his tail and slid along his back.

As soon as the ox came close to the other side of the river, the rat jumped off his back and onto the bank.

'Hooray! I win,' shouted the rat.

'You do indeed,' said the king,' The New Year will be the Year of the Rat.'

The rest of the animals arrived one by one.

'We will name the next 11 years after you,' said the princess kindly.

'Always in this order, Rat, Ox, Tiger, Rabbit, Dragon, Snake, Horse, Ram, Monkey, Rooster, Dog and Pig.'

The 12 animals jumped up and down with excitement and from that day the Chinese have named the New Year after each one of them in turn.

Ganesha, Ganesha!

Sally Scott

Ganesha, Ganesha!

(Children stand in a circle. A child or adult is chosen to stand in the middle and act as a prompt, holding up props related to each verse.)

I am going on holiday.
I am going on holiday.
I need someone to wish me luck,
And help me on my way.

(Children make up their own actions related to going on holiday, for example, packing a case. The prompt holds up a small suitcase.)

Chorus
Ganesha, Ganesha! Help us all today.
Ganesha, Ganesha! Help us on our way.

(Children join hands and skip or dance around in a ring. The prompt holds a Ganesha mask in front of their face.)

I am going to my new school.
I am going to my new school.
I need someone to wish me luck,
And help me on my way.

(Children make up their own actions related to going to school, for example, putting on uniform. The prompt holds up an item of school uniform such as a tie or sweatshirt.)

Chorus
(As above.)

I am going to visit friends.
I am going to visit friends.
I need someone to wish me luck,
And help me on my way.

(Children wave to a friend in the circle. The prompt puts on a hat and scarf to represent an outing to visit friends.)

Chorus
(As above.)

I am going to learn to swim.
I am going to learn to swim.
I need someone to wish me luck,
And help me on my way.

(Children pretend to swim. The prompt holds up a pair of armbands.)

Chorus
(As above.)

Chorus repeat
(As above.)

Ganesha, Ganesha!
How to use this song

Learning objectives

Stepping Stone
Have an awareness of, and show interest and enjoyment in, cultural and religious differences.

Early Learning Goal
Understand that people have different needs, views, cultures and beliefs, that need to be treated with respect. **(PSED)**

Group size
Up to 12 children.

Props
Ganesha mask (see activity ideas); small suitcase; item of familiar school uniform, such as a tie or sweatshirt; child's hat and scarf; pair of armbands.

Sharing the song

Share this song during circle time, especially before a special event such as the end of summer term before children go on holiday, or when older children leave to join a new school. Include the song in planned activities related to themes such as 'festivals', 'celebrations' and 'myself'.

Explain that the song is about Ganesha Chaturthi, the elephant-headed god of wisdom and prosperity. Look at the mask of Ganesha's head. What is special about it? Talk about how Hindus pray to Ganesha to bring them strength and good luck when they move house, go on a journey or try something new.

Listen to the words of the song together to stimulate discussion about the children's personal experiences. How did they feel on their first day at nursery or school?

Decide upon appropriate actions for each verse, emphasising that the children can create individual actions if they wish to, and practise skipping in a circle. Choose someone to be the prompt and invite the children to sit in a circle with the prompt in the middle. Enjoy singing and moving together. Repeat the song several times so that the children can take turns to be the prompt.

Activity ideas

● Explain how Hindus make clay images during the birthday celebrations of Ganesha and suggest that the children make their own Ganesha clay models. **(PSED)**

● Talk about how Ganesha has an elephant's head because Hindus believe that an elephant's strong trunk can move things that are in the way when they do something new. Look at pictures and models of elephants. Try making a model elephant from large recycled materials such as boxes and tubes. Encourage the children to talk about the size and shape of the objects they use. **(MD)**

● Make copies of the elephant head of Ganesha on page 41, mount it on card and cut out the eye holes. Invite the children to add collage materials, such as sequins or shiny fabric scraps, to the surface to decorate the head before cutting around it. Tape a piece of cane to the back of each one so that the children can hold their masks to their faces. Create an additional mask to use as a prop in the song. **(PD)**

Ganesha, Ganesha!

Dance Around the Maypole

Holding tight to our bright ribbons, Holding tight to our bright ribbons,

Holding tight to our bright ribbons, Dance around the maypole.

Sally Scott

Dance Around the Maypole

(Children stand in a circle around a pole secured in a Christmas tree stand, wearing armbands made from ribbons in two contrasting colours, for example, red and yellow, and carrying short lengths of coloured ribbon in the same colours. The coloured armbands alternate around the circle; red, yellow, red, yellow. The children can also wear bells on their ankles or wrists.)

Holding tight to our bright ribbons,
Holding tight to our bright ribbons,
Holding tight to our bright ribbons,
Dance around the maypole.

(All of the children dance around the pole waving their ribbons up in the air.)
Reach under with our bright ribbons,
Reach under with our bright ribbons,
Reach under with our bright ribbons,
Dance around the maypole.

(Children wearing red armbands join their hands high in the air while those wearing yellow armbands dance under the arches they have created waving their ribbons.)
Reach over with our bright ribbons,
Reach over with our bright ribbons,
Reach over with our bright ribbons,
Dance around the maypole.

(Children wearing yellow armbands stand still with their arms by their sides while those wearing red armbands dance in and out of them waving their ribbons over the heads of the standing children.)
Skip around with our bright ribbons,
Skip around with our bright ribbons,
Skip around with our bright ribbons,
Dance around the maypole.

(All of the children skip around the pole holding up their ribbons.)

Dance Around the Maypole
How to use this song

Learning objectives

Stepping Stone
Develop a repertoire of actions by putting a sequence of movements together.

Early Learning Goal
Use their imagination in music and dance. **(CD)**

Group size
12 children.

Props
Pictures of maypoles and maypole dancing; broom handle; Christmas tree stand; short lengths of ribbon in two contrasting colours; jingle bells on ribbons of the same colours.

Sharing the song

Share this song during a music and dance session or as part of May Day celebrations (held on 1 May each year). Include the song in planned activities related to themes such as 'festivals', 'celebrations', 'colours' and 'Summer'.

Show the children the pictures of maypole dancing and talk about traditional celebrations associated with May Day. Explain how dancers weave patterns with the ribbons attached to the maypole as they dance in and out of their friends.

Create a maypole together by standing a broom handle in a Christmas tree stand and weaving ribbon of contrasting colours around the pole. Make coloured armbands by tying a length of ribbon around the top of each child's arm, hand out lengths of ribbon of the same colour and provide jingle bells on ribbons to tie to the children's wrists or ankles.

Explain that holding ribbons tied to a maypole while dancing is quite difficult and that this is an easier dance for them to try. Help them to position themselves so that their coloured armbands alternate around the circle.

Listen to the song together and then enjoy simply dancing in a circle to each verse before adding the suggested actions.

Activity ideas

● Hold a special May Day celebration in your setting with maypole dancing and refreshments. Help the children to make invitations for parents and get parents involved by asking them to set up fundraising stalls. Encourage the children to dress in brightly-coloured clothes for the event. **(PSED)**

● Supply a selection of ribbons of different lengths and invite the children to arrange them into a line with the shortest at one end and the longest at the other. Provide the children with scissors and ask them to try to make them all the same length. Offer help to younger children using scissors if appropriate. **(MD)**

● Attach some narrow ribbons to a short length of dowelling pushed into a yoghurt pot of clay to create a maypole for small-world characters to dance around. Provide a music player and suitable music so that the children can set up miniature May Day celebrations. **(KUW)**

● Supply each child with a copy of the puzzle on page 45 and encourage them to guess which of the ribbons on the illustrated maypole has snapped. Show them how to check their answer by following each ribbon from the hand of the child holding it to the top of the maypole. **(PD)**

Dance Around the Maypole

The Scottish Country Dance

Now find a dance part-ner, stand in the mi-ddle. Link arms to-ge-ther and stamp both your feet. Now skip round the room with a hop and a jump. Find a new part-ner and dance it a-gain!

Sally Scott

The Scottish Country Dance

(Children find partners before starting to dance so that an adult can help them. They are dressed in kilts.)

Now find a dance partner, stand in the middle.

(The children stand together in the centre of the room in pairs holding hands.)

Link arms together and stamp both your feet.

(The children link one of their partner's arms and stamp their feet.)

Now skip round the room with a hop and a jump,

(The children dance around the room in pairs, still linking arms.)

Find a new partner and dance it again!

(The children stop dancing and find a new partner. It may be necessary to pause the music and help them with this.)

Now find a dance partner, stand in the middle.
Link arms together and stamp both your feet.
Now skip round the room with a hop and a jump.
Find a new partner and dance it again!

(As first verse.)

Now find a dance partner, stand in the middle.
Link arms together and stamp both your feet.
Now skip round the room with a hop and a jump.
Find a new partner and dance it again!

(As first verse.)

The Scottish Country Dance
How to use this song

Sharing the song

Share this song during a music and dance session, or as a planned activity to support aspects of themes such as 'Scotland', 'musical instruments', 'all about me' and 'clothes'.

Listen to the song together and explain that this is a Scottish dance. Look at the pictures of traditional dress and some of the instruments used in a Scottish dance band. Look at the children's kilts and the kilts you have made and explain that the design is known as tartan. Talk about how the dancers follow sequences, changing partners and moving around the dance floor in time to the music.

Play the instrumental version of the song and invite the children to dance around by themselves to become familiar with the music and the rhythm. Now ask them to choose a partner and demonstrate how to link arms and skip around the room. Practise this until the children are comfortable with moving alongside someone else and then play the song with the suggested actions. Suggest that the children invent moves of their own and put them together to form a new dance.

Activity ideas

● Introduce the word 'ceilidh' and explain that this is an exciting occasion when Scottish people come together to enjoy traditional dancing. Hold your own ceilidh with the children wearing kilts and dancing to a variety of Scottish dance music. **(PSED)**

● Talk about traditional Scottish foods, such as broth, oatcakes, stovies (leftover potato and vegetable dish), shortbread, haggis and porridge, and follow a simple recipe to make some Scotch pancakes to share at snack time. **(CLL)**

● Collect different tartan patterns on wrapping paper, fabric and clothes and talk about how some families or 'clans' in Scotland have their own tartan. Look at the patterns and colours in the examples. Try creating a tartan pattern using brushes of different widths to paint horizontal and vertical stripes on a coloured paper background. **(MD)**

● Look at a map of the British Isles and outline the location of Scotland. Look for features on the map such as large lochs, mountains and islands off the coast. **(KUW)**

● Talk about the legend of Nessie, the monster that is said to live in the deep water of Loch Ness. Mount copies of page 49 on card and invite the children to colour in the picture of Nessie. Cut out Nessie's head and attach it to a thin strip of thick card. Push the card through the slot on the sheet so that Nessie's head can move in and out of the water when the children pull the strips fron behind. **(CD)**

The Scottish Country Dance

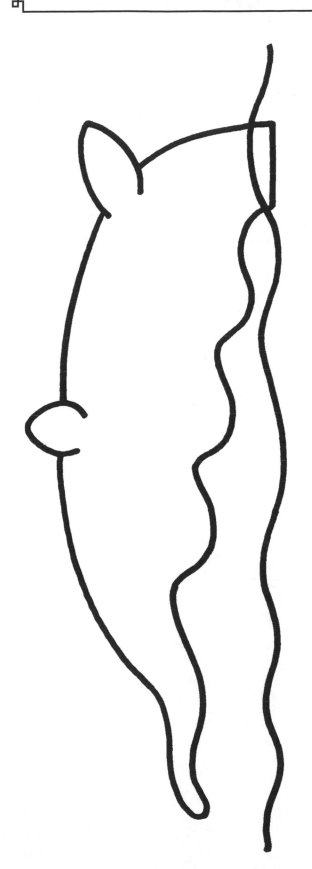

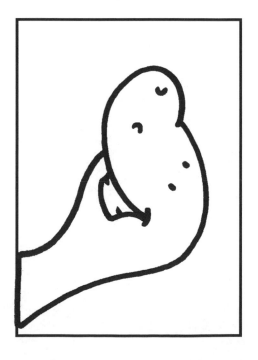

Festivals

Let's All Make Some Pancakes

Sally Scott

Let's All Make Some Pancakes

Let's all make some pancakes.
Let's all make some pancakes.
(Toss them! Toss them!
In the pan.)
*The children pretend to toss imaginary pancakes up
into the air.*

Measure out some flour.
Measure out some milk.
*(The children pretend to measure out the
ingredients.)*

Mix them! Mix them!
In the bowl.
(The children pretend to stir the mixture in the bowl.)

Next, crack in an egg.
Add some salt and pepper.
*(The children pretend to crack an egg and shake
some salt and pepper into a bowl.)*

Mix them! Mix them!
In the bowl.
(The children pretend to stir the mixture in the bowl.)

Help me pour the mixture,
In the frying pan.
*(The children pretend to pour the pancake batter
into a frying pan.)*

Fry it! Fry it!
In the pan.
(The children pretend to fry a pancake in a frying pan.)

Let's all make some pancakes.
Let's all make some pancakes.
Toss them! Toss them!
In the pan.
(As first verse.)

Let's All Make Some Pancakes
How to use this song

Learning objectives:

Stepping Stone
Know that information can be retrieved from books and computers.

Early Learning Goal
Know that print carries meaning and, in English, is read from left to right and top to bottom. **(CLL)**

Group size
Six children.

Props
The children's book about their pancake-making session (see activity idea).

Sharing the song

Share this song before a pancake-making session, particularly on Shrove Tuesday, or after reading the traditional story 'The Enormous Pancake'. Include the song in planned activities related to themes such as 'food', 'changes' and 'festivals'.

Remind the children of their pancake-making session and share the book they have made following the sequence of their actions (see activity ideas). Talk to the children about each stage of the pancake-making procedure, encouraging them to use appropriate language of time and sequence by asking them questions about what they did 'first', 'next' and 'last'.

Read out the words of the song and point out the 'doing' words such as 'toss', 'measure', 'mix', 'pour', 'crack', 'add' and 'fry'. Encourage the children to think of appropriate movements to represent these actions and practise them together. Sing the song together and include the children's chosen actions as you sing.

Activity ideas

● Look at the recipe on page 53 and search books and the internet to find pancake recipes and ideas for fillings. Make comparisons between them. Are the ingredients always the same? **(CLL)**

● Use play dough to create pancakes and introduce mathematical language to describe their size, shape, weight and thickness. Ask questions to encourage simple problem solving, for example, 'My pancake is quite thin. Can you make a thicker one?' or 'Can you make the pancake on this side of the scales weigh the same as the one on the other by adding some more play dough?' **(MD)**

● Make a copy of the pancake recipe on page 53, mount it on card and laminate it for protection. Follow the step-by-step instructions to make some pancakes and encourage the children to choose their own fillings. Keep the pancakes warm in an oven and share them at snack time. Remember to check for any food allergies before allowing the children to taste food. **(KUW)**

● Create pancake shapes from scraps of oatmeal coloured vinyl flooring and suggest that the children try to toss them outdoors with toy frying pans or plastic tennis racquets. Leave some of them in the home area to extend role play. **(PD)**

● Take photographs of the children at each stage of making pancakes. Use these photographs, along with the children's drawings, to create a book about pancake making. Invite the children to suggest captions and scribe for them if necessary. Use the book as a prop to help the children to recall how they made their pancakes before singing the song. **(CD)**

Let's All Make Some Pancakes

Sieve 100g flour and a pinch of salt into a bowl.

Crack two eggs into a jug and whisk with a balloon whisk. Measure 300ml milk into another jug.

Make a well shape in the centre of the flour and pour in some of the egg mixture and some of the milk.

Whisk the liquid into the flour. Gradually add the rest of the milk and whisk to form a thick batter. Pour the batter into a jug.

Heat a frying pan away from the children and pour in two tablespoons of the batter. Tilt the frying pan around to coat the surface with the batter.

Cook the pancake for about a minute and then turn it over and cook the other side.

Put the pancake onto a plate and spread the chosen filling over it. Roll it up and keep it warm in the oven. Enjoy the pancakes at snack time.

Suggested fillings:
Lemon juice and sugar.
Syrup.
Grated cheese and chopped ham.
Cooked sliced mushrooms and crème fraiche.

Ethiopian New Year

Sally Scott

Ethiopian New Year

*(The children dress in costumes of their choice.
Four of them form a reggae band playing drums.)*

Today is Ethiopian New Year.
Today is Ethiopian New Year.
We're going to have a street party with
our friends.
Yes, it's Ethiopian New Year!

*(All of the children, except the reggae band, dance
around the room, moving to the music as they
sing.)*

Today is Ethiopian New Year.
Today is Ethiopian New Year.
We're going to listen to the reggae band.
Yes, it's Ethiopian New Year!

*(The children stand and listen to the reggae band,
clapping and singing in time to the music.)*

Today is Ethiopian New Year.
Today is Ethiopian New Year.
We're going to shout and sing loud with
our friends.
Yes, it's Ethiopian New Year!

*(All of the children, except the reggae band, move
to the music and sing loudly. The band play their
drums and shout and cheer.)*

Today is Ethiopian New Year.
Today is Ethiopian New Year.
We're going to play some fun games
with our friends.
Yes, it's Ethiopian New Year!

*(All of the children, except the reggae band, join
hands in a circle and dance and sing.)*

Ethiopian New Year
How to use this song

Learning objectives:

Stepping Stone
Listen to favourite nursery rhymes, stories and songs. Join in with repeated refrains, anticipating key events and important phrases.

Early Learning Goal
Listen with enjoyment, and respond to stories, songs and other music, rhymes and poems. **(CLL)**

Group size
12 children.

Props
Costumes and four drums (see activity ideas).

Sharing the song

Share this song during movement and dance sessions, or to celebrate the Ethiopian New Year on 11 September. Include it in planned activities related to themes such as 'sound', 'seasons', 'countries of the world' and 'festivals'.

Explain to the children that the Ethiopian New Year is celebrated at the end of the long rains when flowers are everywhere. Children call at their friends and neighbours' houses to give out garlands of flowers and painted pictures. In the evening, families light bonfires and enjoy parties with celebratory singing and dancing.

Listen to the instrumental version of the song and talk about how Rastafarian reggae bands began with the African tradition of drumming and chanting. Choose four children to play the drums while the others clap and chant an appropriate word, such as 'reggae', in time to the music.

Invite the children to dress in costumes of their choice and join in with the vocal version of the song, following the suggested actions.

Activity ideas

● Enjoy listening and moving freely to some reggae music, for example, the CDs 'Reggae for Kids' and 'More Reggae for Kids' **(www.rasrecords.com/reggaeforkids/). (PSED)**

● Create African style robes from long T-shirts in the Rastafarian colours of red, green or yellow. Encourage the children to add designs using fabric paint in the same colours. Ask parents to donate brightly coloured knitted beret style hats to create traditional 'tams' for the children to wear. Leave the clothes in the home area for role play, and use as costumes for the song. **(CLL)**

● Create patterns using the Rastafarian colours of red, green and yellow, for example, painting stripes or threading beads in regular sequences. **(MD)**

● Follow the recipe for banana bread on page 57 and share it as part of your Ethiopian celebrations. Encourage the children to measure the ingredients and observe changes throughout the cooking process. Remember to check for any allergies before allowing the children to taste food. **(KUW)**

● Make some drums from baby milk tins or old plastic paper bins. Invite the children to cover the outside with a mixture of PVA glue and paint in their choice of red, green or yellow. When the paint has dried add designs in the remaining two colours. Put the lids back on the tins or create a drum skin from stretched polythene tightly secured around the side of the bin with string. Use the drums to form a reggae band. **(PD)**

Ethiopian New Year

Banana bread recipe

Ingredients
115g sunflower margarine
1 tsp bicarbonate of soda
225g wholemeal flour
2 eggs
3 ripe bananas
40ml milk

Utensils
Large mixing bowl, three small bowls, sieve, scales, fork or balloon whisk, tablespoon, teaspoon, wooden spoon, measuring jug, small loaf tin, cooling rack.

Hints
- Make sure that the bananas are very ripe.
- Involve the children as much as possible in the process.
- Do not let the children touch the raw eggs.
- Make sure that the children wash their hands before and after the session.
- Make sure an adult completes the actions marked (A).

Step by step
- Heat the oven to 180C, 350F or gas mark 4. (A)
- Grease a loaf tin with some of the margarine.
- Beat the margarine in a bowl until it is soft and creamy.
- Sieve the bicarbonate of soda and the flour into a small bowl.
- Crack the eggs (A) and beat them in another small bowl.
- Gradually, add the flour mixture and the eggs to the margarine alternately.
- Peel the bananas and mash them in a bowl.
- Stir the mashed bananas into the bread mixture.
- Add the milk.
- Put the mixture into the loaf tin with a large spoon.
- Bake for around an hour and a half. (A)
- Turn out the loaf onto a cooling rack. (A)
- Serve the loaf in slices at snack time.

Light the Way Home

Knock, knock at num - ber one, here is your can - dle.

Light a can-dle for Ra-ma and Si-ta, Light a can-dle to - day.

One can - dle bur - ning, shi - ning in the win - dow.

Light a can-dle for Ra-ma and Si-ta, light the wa - y home!

Sally Scott

Light the Way Home

(Ten children stand in a line behind a bench wearing numbered tabards in order from one to ten and carrying clay diva lamps. Card numbers are arranged along the bench in front of the children in the same order. One child walks along carrying a basket of ten tea lights.)

Knock, knock at number one, here is your candle.
Light a candle for Rama and Sita,
Light a candle today.

(The 'candle distributor' pretends to knock on the door of the first house and hands the child a tea light.)

One candle burning, shining in the window.
Light a candle for Rama and Sita,
Light the way home!

(The child pretends to light the candle and puts it in the diva lamp on the bench beside the appropriate numeral.)

Knock, knock at number two, here is your candle.
Light a candle for Rama and Sita,
Light a candle today.

(The 'candle distributor' pretends to knock on the door of the second house and hands the child a tea light.)

Two candles burning, shining in the window.
Light a candle for Rama and Sita,
Light the way home!

(As first verse. Continue with each verse until number ten.)

Knock, knock at number ten, here is your candle.
Light a candle for Rama and Sita,
Light a candle today.

(The 'candle distributor' pretends to knock on the door of the last house and hands the child a tea light.)

Ten candles burning, shining in the window.
Light a candle for Rama and Sita,
Light the way home!

(As first verse.)

Light the Way home
How to use this song

Learning objectives

Stepping Stone
Enjoy joining in with number rhymes and songs.

Early Learning Goal
Count reliably up to ten everyday objects. **(MD)**

Group size
11 children.

Props
Tabards or sport bibs numbered from one to ten; small basket; ten tea lights; bench; children's clay diva lamps.

Sharing the song

Share this song during circle time to extend mathematical development, or during the Hindu festival of Diwali (the date varies but is at the end of October or beginning of November each year. Diwali will be celebrated on 26 October in 2006). Include it in planned activities related to aspects of themes such as 'seasons', 'opposites (dark and light)', 'numbers' and 'festivals'.

Before singing the song read the story of Rama and Sita on page 61. Explain that the song is about this story and suggest that the children pretend to be in their houses lighting the way for Rama and Sita's return.

Choose a child to be the candle distributor and supply them with a basket. With the children, count ten candles and put them into the basket. Supply the other children with numbered tabards or bibs and ask them to sit on the floor. Talk about how houses in a street are numbered in order. Which number will come first? Ask the child wearing number 'one' to stand behind one end of the bench.

Invite the children to take their places one by one by saying, 'What number comes after one?', and so on, up to ten. Hand the children their diva lamps (see activity ideas) and arrange card numbers from one to ten along the bench.

Sing the song together while the candle distributor walks along the street giving out a candle during each verse.

Activity ideas

● After singing the song, when all of the diva lamps are in a row on the bench, invite the children to sit further back. Light the candles and turn off the lights to create atmosphere while reading the story of Rama and Sita on page 61 to the children. **(CLL)**

● Look at some pictures of diva lamps with the children. Invite them to make their own lamps from clay, to use as a prop in the song. Encourage the children to check the size to make sure that a tea light fits into the centre of their diva lamp by pushing one into the clay while it is wet and then removing it to form a well. **(MD)**

● Talk to the children about what we do to see in the dark. Encourage discussion about electric lights in our homes and streets and battery operated torches. Compare these to the candle light in the story of Rama and Sita. Why are torches safer than candles? Take apart a torch and show the children how it works. **(KUW)**

● Talk about the tradition of drawing Rangoli patterns in the entrances to Hindu homes to welcome the goddess Lakshmi during Diwali. Ask the childen to draw some simple geometric patterns on the ground outdoors with coloured chalk, or paint patterns indoors to display in the entrance of your setting. **(PD)**

Light the Way Home

The story of Rama and Sita
Retold by Jean Evans

Once long ago, in a faraway place called Ayodhya, there lived a prince called Rama. Prince Rama loved his wife Sita and his favourite brother Lakshman very much.

Rama's father was getting old and wanted him to be the next king but his wife, the queen, did not agree with him. The king wanted to please his wife so he sent Rama and Sita far away from their home into a thick jungle and told them to stay there. Lakshman was unhappy that his brother was leaving and decided to go too, because he loved his brother Rama so much.

The three friends lived happily in the jungle for many years, until one day a wicked demon with ten heads stole Sita and took her to his palace on the island of Lanka. Rama and Lakshman were very sad because they missed Sita. They searched everywhere for her but could not find her.

A strong monkey warrior, Hanuman, decided to help them. He could travel like lightning, jumping over the treetops with his long arms and legs. He began to look for Sita. He looked here and he looked there and soon he spotted her sitting in the garden of the wicked demon's palace. He called to his monkey friends and they made a bridge of stones to the island so that Rama and Lakshman could climb over it and rescue Sita.

They were all so pleased to see one another again and Rama decided that it was time to take Sita to his home in Ayodhya. They travelled through the thick jungle until they saw some twinkling lights in the distance. 'Look over there, Sita', said Rama, 'Can you see the lights shining?' The people of Ayodhya had lit oil lamps called divas and put them in their windows to light the way for Rama and Sita. There was great excitement as they appeared, following the lights along the way. All the streets were decorated, and colourful fireworks lit the sky. People clapped and cheered to see that Rama had arrived safely at home with Sita.

Today, Hindu people celebrate the festival of Diwali by lighting their homes with diva lamps and fairy lights. They have parties with special food, new clothes and presents and everyone is happy.

Kodomo-no-hi

My carp kite flies in the sky, in the sky, in the sky.

My carp kite flies in the sky, Ko - do - mo - no - hi!

Sally Scott

Kodomo-no-hi

(The children stand in a circle well away from one another holding their carp kites.)

My carp kite flies in the sky,
In the sky, in the sky.
My carp kite flies in the sky,
Kodomo-no-hi!

(The children wave their kites around above their heads.)

My carp kite floats up and down,
Up and down, up and down.
My carp kite floats up and down,
Kodomo-no-hi!

(The children make their kites float up and down.)

My carp kite spins round and round,
Round and round, round and round.
My carp kite spins round and round,
Kodomo-no-hi!

(The children make their kites spin round and round.)

My carp kite floats to the ground,
To the ground, to the ground.
My carp kite floats to the ground,
Kodomo-no-hi!

(The children make their kites float near the ground.)

Kodomo-no-hi
How to use this song

Learning objectives

Stepping Stone
Show interest by sustained construction activity or by talking about shapes or arrangements.

Early Learning Goal
Use language such as 'circle' or 'bigger' to describe the shape and size of solids and flat shapes. **(MD)**

Group size
Up to eight children.

Props
The children's carp kites (see activity ideas).

Sharing the song

Share this song outside on a windy day, or to celebrate the Japanese festival of Kodomo-no-hi on 5 May. Include it in planned activities related to themes such as 'colours', 'weather', 'families' and 'festivals'.

Talk to the children about how the festival of Kodomo-no-hi is known as Children's Day, when Japanese people celebrate the health and happiness of children. Describe the tradition of flying carp-shaped kites outside houses, with several kites of different sizes fastened to a long bamboo pole to represent the members of the family who live there.

Introduce the song by saying that it is about the carp kites that the children have made. Look at the different kites, using mathematical language to talk about their size and shape, and introduce appropriate positional language as the children practise moving them up, down and around before singing the song. Emphasise the need to stand well away from one another so that no

child is hurt by the moving canes supporting the kites.

Activity ideas

● Discuss the tradition of making carp kites in different sizes to represent family members. Create a carp kite (see activity below) for each member of their immediate family, with longer tails for adults and smaller tails for children. Discuss family differences with sensitivity. Tie each family of kites to a garden cane and push it into a patch of soil or large outdoor plant pot. **(PSED)**

● Create a carp windsock from a tube of tissue paper and some streamers. Hang it up outdoors to observe the direction and strength of the wind. **(KUW)**

● Run around outdoors on a windy day holding streamers in the air. Talk about how the wind feels and refer to changes in the body after exercise. **(PD)**

● Make carp kites to use as props during the song. Cut out a simple card outline of the head and body of a carp and invite the children to decorate both sides with sparkling collage materials, such as sequins and glitter, to represent shiny fish scales. Attach long streamers of coloured tissue to the back to form a tail. Tie the front of the carp to a short length of cane so that the children can hold up their kites and wave them around. **(CD)**